Roll of Thunder, Hear My Cry

A guide for the novel by Mildred D. Taylor
Great Works Author: Charles Aracich

SHELL EDUCATION

Publishing Credits

Robin Erickson, *Production Director;* Lee Aucoin, *Creative Director;*
Timothy J. Bradley, *Illustration Manager;* Emily R. Smith, M.A.Ed., *Editorial
Director;* Amber Goff, *Editorial Assistant;* Don Tran, *Production Supervisor;*
Corinne Burton, M.A.Ed., *Publisher*

Image Credits

Cover Fredy Thuerig/cholder/Shutterstock

Standards

© 2007 Teachers of English to Speakers of Other Languages, Inc. (TESOL)
© 2007 Board of Regents of the University of Wisconsin System. World-Class Instructional Design and Assessment (WIDA).
© Copyright 2010. National Governors Association Center for Best Practices and Council of Chief State School Officers.
All rights reserved

Shell Education

5301 Oceanus Drive
Huntington Beach, CA 92649-1030
http://www.shelleducation.com
ISBN 978-1-4258-8987-6
© 2014 Shell Educational Publishing, Inc.
Printed in USA. WOR004

Table of Contents

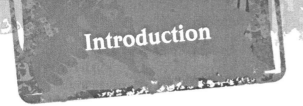

How to Use This Literature Guide

Today's standards demand rigor and relevance in the reading of complex texts. The units in this series guide teachers in a rich and deep exploration of worthwhile works of literature for classroom study. The most rigorous instruction can also be interesting and engaging!

Many current strategies for effective literacy instruction have been incorporated into these instructional guides for literature. Throughout the units, text-dependent questions are used to determine comprehension of the book as well as student interpretation of the vocabulary words. The books chosen for the series are complex and exemplars of carefully crafted works of literature. Close reading is used throughout the units to guide students toward revisiting the text and using textual evidence to respond to prompts orally and in writing. Students must analyze the story elements in multiple assignments for each section of the book. All of these strategies work together to rigorously guide students through their study of literature.

The next few pages will make clear how to use this guide for a purposeful and meaningful literature study. Each section of this guide is set up in the same way to make it easier for you to implement the instruction in your classroom.

Theme Thoughts

The great works of literature used throughout this series have important themes that have been relevant to people for many years. Many of the themes will be discussed during the various sections of this instructional guide. However, it would also benefit students to have independent time to think about the key themes of the novel.

Before students begin reading, have them complete *Pre-Reading Theme Thoughts* (page 13). This graphic organizer will allow students to think about the themes outside the context of the story. They'll have the opportunity to evaluate statements based on important themes and defend their opinions. Be sure to have students keep their papers for comparison to the *Post-Reading Theme Thoughts* (page 64). This graphic organizer is similar to the pre-reading activity. However, this time, students will be answering the questions from the point of view of one of the characters of the novel. They have to think about how the character would feel about each statement and defend their thoughts. To conclude the activity, have students compare what they thought about the themes before the novel to what the characters discovered during the story.

How to Use This Literature Guide *(cont.)*

Vocabulary

Each teacher overview page has definitions and sentences about how key vocabulary words are used in the section. These words should be introduced and discussed with students. There are two student vocabulary activity pages in each section. On the first page, students are asked to define the ten words chosen by the author of this unit. On the second page in most sections, each student will select at least eight words that he or she finds interesting or difficult. For each section, choose one of these pages for your students to complete. With either assignment, you may want to have students get into pairs to discuss the meanings of the words. Allow students to use reference guides to define the words. Monitor students to make sure the definitions they have found are accurate and relate to how the words are used in the text.

On some of the vocabulary student pages, students are asked to answer text-related questions about the vocabulary words. The following question stems will help you create your own vocabulary questions if you'd like to extend the discussion.

- How does this word describe _____'s character?
- In what ways does this word relate to the problem in this story?
- How does this word help you understand the setting?
- In what ways is this word related to the story's solution?
- Describe how this word supports the novel's theme of . . . .
- What visual images does this word bring to your mind?
- For what reasons might the author have chosen to use this particular word?

At times, more work with the words will help students understand their meanings. The following quick vocabulary activities are a good way to further study the words.

- Have students practice their vocabulary and writing skills by creating sentences and/or paragraphs in which multiple vocabulary words are used correctly and with evidence of understanding.
- Students can play vocabulary concentration. Students make a set of cards with the words and a separate set of cards with the definitions. Then, students lay the cards out on the table and play concentration. The goal of the game is to match vocabulary words with their definitions.
- Students can create word journal entries about the words. Students choose words they think are important and then describe why they think each word is important within the book.

How to Use This Literature Guide (cont.)

Analyzing the Literature

After students have read each section, hold small-group or whole-class discussions. Questions are written at two levels of complexity to allow you to decide which questions best meet the needs of your students. The Level 1 questions are typically less abstract than the Level 2 questions. Level 1 is indicated by a square, while Level 2 is indicated by a triangle.

These questions focus on the various story elements, such as character, setting, and plot. Student pages are provided if you want to assign these questions for individual student work before your group discussion. Be sure to add further questions as your students discuss what they've read. For each question, a few key points are provided for your reference as you discuss the novel with students.

Reader Response

In today's classrooms, there are often great readers who are below average writers. So much time and energy is spent in classrooms getting students to read on grade level, that little time is left to focus on writing skills. To help teachers include more writing in their daily literacy instruction, each section of this guide has a literature-based reader response prompt. Each of the three genres of writing is used in the reader responses within this guide: narrative, informative/explanatory, and opinion/argument. Students have a choice between two prompts for each reader response. One response requires students to make connections between the reading and their own lives. The other prompt requires students to determine text-to-text connections or connections within the text.

Close Reading the Literature

Within each section, students are asked to closely reread a short section of text. Since some versions of the novels have different page numbers, the selections are described by chapter and location, along with quotations to guide the readers. After each close reading, there are text-dependent questions to be answered by students.

Encourage students to read each question one at a time and then go back to the text and discover the answer. Work with students to ensure that they use the text to determine their answers rather than making unsupported inferences. Once students have answered the questions, discuss what they discovered. Suggested answers are provided in the answer key.

How to Use This Literature Guide (cont.)

Close Reading the Literature (cont.)

The generic, open-ended stems below can be used to write your own text-dependent questions if you would like to give students more practice.

- Give evidence from the text to support . . . .
- Justify your thinking using text evidence about . . . .
- Find evidence to support your conclusions about . . . .
- What text evidence helps the reader understand . . . ?
- Use the book to tell why _____ happens.
- Based on events in the story, ...
- Use text evidence to describe why . . . .

Making Connections

The activities in this section help students make cross-curricular connections to writing, mathematics, science, social studies, or the fine arts. In some of these lessons, students are asked to use the author as a mentor. The writing in the novel models a skill for them that they can then try to emulate. Students may also be asked to look for examples of language conventions within the novel. Each of these types of activities requires higher-order thinking skills from students.

Creating with the Story Elements

It is important to spend time discussing the common story elements in literature. Understanding the characters, setting, and plot can increase students' comprehension and appreciation of the story. If teachers discuss these elements daily, students will more likely internalize the concepts and look for the elements in their independent reading. Another very important reason for focusing on the story elements is that students will be better writers if they think about how the stories they read are constructed.

Students are given three options for working with the story elements. They are asked to create something related to the characters, setting, or plot of the novel. Students are given choice on this activity so that they can decide to complete the activity that most appeals to them. Different multiple intelligences are used so that the activities are diverse and interesting to all students.

How to Use This Literature Guide (cont.)

Culminating Activity

This open-ended, cross-curricular activity requires higher-order thinking and allows for a creative product. Students will enjoy getting the chance to share what they have discovered through reading the novel. Be sure to allow them enough time to complete the activity at school or home.

Comprehension Assessment

The questions in this section are modeled after current standardized tests to help students analyze what they've read and prepare for tests they may see in their classrooms. The questions are dependent on the text and require critical-thinking skills to answer.

Response to Literature

The final post-reading activity is an essay based on the text that also requires further research by students. This is a great way to extend this book into other curricular areas. A suggested rubric is provided for teacher reference.

Correlation to the Standards

Shell Education is committed to producing educational materials that are research and standards based. In this effort, we have correlated all of our products to the academic standards of all 50 United States, the District of Columbia, the Department of Defense Dependents Schools, and all Canadian provinces.

Purpose and Intent of Standards

Standards are designed to focus instruction and guide adoption of curricula. Standards are statements that describe the criteria necessary for students to meet specific academic goals. They define the knowledge, skills, and content students should acquire at each level. Standards are also used to develop standardized tests to evaluate students' academic progress. Teachers are required to demonstrate how their lessons meet standards. Standards are used in the development of all of our products, so educators can be assured they meet high academic standards.

How To Find Standards Correlations

To print a customized correlation report of this product for your state, visit our website at http://www.shelleducation.com and follow the online directions. If you require assistance in printing correlation reports, please contact Customer Service at 1-877-777-3450.

Correlation to the Standards (cont.)

Standards Correlation Chart

The lessons in this guide were written to support the Common Core College and Career Readiness Anchor Standards. This chart indicates which sections of this guide address the anchor standards.

Common Core College and Career Readiness Anchor Standard	Section
CCSS.ELA-Literacy.CCRA.R.1—Read closely to determine what the text says explicitly and to make logical inferences from it; cite specific textual evidence when writing or speaking to support conclusions drawn from the text.	Vocabulary Sections 1–5; Culminating Activity
CCSS.ELA-Literacy.CCRA.R.2—Determine central ideas or themes of a text and analyze their development; summarize the key supporting details and ideas.	Pre-Reading Theme Thoughts; Culminating Activity
CCSS.ELA-Literacy.CCRA.R.3—Analyze how and why individuals, events, or ideas develop and interact over the course of a text.	Analyzing the Literature Sections 1–5; Culminating Activity
CCSS.ELA-Literacy.CCRA.R.4—Interpret words and phrases as they are used in a text, including determining technical, connotative, and figurative meanings, and analyze how specific word choices shape meaning or tone.	Vocabulary Sections 1–5
CCSS.ELA-Literacy.CCRA.R.5—Analyze the structure of texts, including how specific sentences, paragraphs, and larger portions of the text (e.g., a section, a chapter) relate to each other and the whole.	Analyzing the Literature Sections 1–5
CCSS.ELA-Literacy.CCRA.R.10—Read and comprehend complex literary and informational texts independently and proficiently.	Entire Unit
CCSS.ELA-Literacy.CCRA.W.1—Write arguments to support claims in an analysis of substantive topics or texts using valid reasoning and relevant and sufficient evidence.	Close Reading the Literature Sections 1–5; Reader Response Sections 1, 3–4; Making Connections Sections 1–5
CCSS.ELA-Literacy.CCRA.W.2—Write informative/explanatory texts to examine and convey complex ideas and information clearly and accurately through the effective selection, organization, and analysis of content.	Analyzing the Literature Sections 1–5; Reader Response Sections 2, 4–5; Culminating Activity

Correlation to the Standards (cont.)

Standards Correlation Chart (cont.)

Common Core College and Career Readiness Anchor Standard	Section
CCSS.ELA-Literacy.CCRA.W.3—Write narratives to develop real or imagined experiences or events using effective technique, well-chosen details and well-structured event sequences.	Reader Response Sections 2–3, 5
CCSS.ELA-Literacy.CCRA.W.4—Produce clear and coherent writing in which the development, organization, and style are appropriate to task, purpose, and audience.	Analyzing the Literature Sections 1–5; Creating with the Story Elements Sections 1–5
CCSS.ELA-Literacy.CCRA.L.1—Demonstrate command of the conventions of standard English grammar and usage when writing or speaking.	Analyzing the Literature Sections 1–5; Close Reading the Literature Sections 1–5
CCSS.ELA-Literacy.CCRA.L.3—Apply knowledge of language to understand how language functions in different contexts, to make effective choices for meaning or style, and to comprehend more fully when reading or listening.	Analyzing the Literature Sections 1–5; Comprehension Assessment
CCSS.ELA-Literacy.CCRA.L.4—Determine or clarify the meaning of unknown and multiple-meaning words and phrases by using context clues, analyzing meaningful word parts, and consulting general and specialized reference materials, as appropriate.	Vocabulary Sections 1–5
CCSS.ELA-Literacy.CCRA.L.6—Acquire and use accurately a range of general academic and domain-specific words and phrases sufficient for reading, writing, speaking, and listening at the college and career readiness level; demonstrate independence in gathering vocabulary knowledge when encountering an unknown term important to comprehension or expression.	Vocabulary Sections 1–5

TESOL and WIDA Standards

The lessons in this book promote English language development for English language learners. The following TESOL and WIDA English Language Development Standards are addressed through the activities in this book:

- **Standard 1:** English language learners communicate for social and instructional purposes within the school setting.

- **Standard 2:** English language learners communicate information, ideas and concepts necessary for academic success in the content area of language arts.

About the Author—Mildred D. Taylor

Mildred DeLois Taylor was born on September 13, 1943, in Jackson, Mississippi. She spent only a short time there and then moved to Toledo, Ohio, where she spent most of her childhood. She graduated from the University of Toledo in 1965. After graduating, Taylor spent a few years teaching history in Ethiopia while working for the Peace Corps.

Taylor's first book, *Song of the Trees*, was published in 1975. The book introduces the Logan family and is narrated by Cassie, the family's young daughter. *Roll of Thunder, Hear My Cry* was Taylor's second novel. It won the Newbery Medal in 1977. Her third book, *Let the Circle Be Unbroken*, published in 1982, continues the journey of the Logan family as Cassie is now 14 years old. Taylor also wrote two short novels, *Mississippi Bridge* (1987) and *The Friendship* (1990), which also deal with the exploits of the Logan family.

In 1995, Taylor published the fourth book centering on the Logan family titled *The Well*. A prequel to her other novels, this story centers on the Logan family when they decide to share the water from their family well during a lengthy drought. This story is narrated by a young David Logan, Cassie's father.

In 2001, Taylor wrote her fifth and final book about the Logan family. Titled *The Land*, this story takes place before all the others in the series. It centers on Paul Logan, Cassie's grandfather, who grows up as a freed slave after the Civil War.

Possible Texts for Text Comparisons

Other books that can be used to compare and contrast this authors writing style include: *The Land*, *The Well*, *Song of the Trees*, *Let the Circle Be Unbroken*, *Mississippi Bridge*, *The Friendship*, *The Gold Cadillac*, and *The Road to Memphis*.

Note Regarding Subject Matter of This Novel

Roll of Thunder, Hear My Cry takes place during a volatile time in American history. In this novel, there are graphic scenes of violence against African American characters. Teachers need to be aware of the violence in the book and be prepared to discuss what happens in each episode. It is suggested that teachers read ahead of their students and introduce the disturbing moments of the book beforehand as much as possible to prepare students for the events. Furthermore, the many instances of nonviolent yet still abusive treatment of characters should likewise be discussed, particularly pertaining to the abusive ways in which African American characters are often spoken to.

Book Summary of *Roll of Thunder, Hear My Cry*

Roll of Thunder, Hear My Cry is the second of Mildred Taylor's novels about the Logan family. This novel is set near Vicksburg, Mississippi, in 1933. During the Great Depression, the Logan family struggles to make ends meet financially, while also dealing with prejudice and injustices from the local white community. Cassie Logan, a nine-year-old girl, is the narrator of the story. Cassie lives with her brothers Stacey, Christopher John, and Little Man in a small home with their mother, father, and grandmother. Their home is on a small piece of land that the family owns. Cassie's grandfather bought the land and the family works very hard not to lose it.

The story mostly follows the children as they experience life in this racially segregated region. Cassie experiences personal insults and prejudices from white people in the community. She then begins to question the fairness and necessity of it all.

At the beginning of the book, we learn that angry members of a white family have attacked an African American family in the area. During this attack, one man dies while another is badly burned. The guilty members of the Wallace family are never punished for these crimes.

In response, the Logans organize a boycott of the supply store owned by the Wallace family. The Logans encourage others to follow the boycott and shop in nearby Vicksburg. However, the Logan family is soon threatened by the Wallace family as well as a wealthy landowner named Mr. Granger.

One night, supporters of the Wallaces attack Papa, Stacey, and a friend named Mr. Morrison. On a return trip from Vicksburg where they were buying supplies, Papa is nearly killed. Papa, who is now injured with a broken leg, can no longer work at his job on the railroad. Mama has also lost her job as a teacher, and the family begins to find it difficult to make ends meet.

The story ends with a near lynching of a friend of the family who is framed by some white teens in the community. To distract those involved in this senseless act, Papa sets fire to the cotton plants on his farm. The members of the community try desperately to save the crops and prevent the fire from spreading to other land.

Cross-Curricular Connection

This book can be used during a unit on the lives of African Americans in the 1930s. Many of the events take place during the beginning of the twentieth century, years after the Civil War has ended. The ways in which many African Americans are treated during this time are clearly illustrated and provide insight into the struggles that many people of the time endured.

Possible Texts for Text Sets

- Spinelli, Jerry. *Maniac Magee*. Little, Brown Books for Young Readers, 1999.
- Curtis, Christopher Paul. *Bud, Not Buddy*. Laurel Leaf, 2004.

Name _____

Date _____

Pre-Reading Theme Thoughts

Directions: Read each of the statements in the first column. Decide if you agree or disagree with the statements. Record your opinion by marking an X in Agree or Disagree for each statement. Explain your choices in the third column. There are no right or wrong answers.

Statement	Agree	Disagree	Explain Your Answer
You can always count on your family.			
Owning land is a symbol of independence.			
Sometimes you have to suffer to learn.			
It is wrong to treat people unfairly based on the color of their skin.			

Vocabulary Overview

Ten key words from this section are provided below with definitions and sentences about how the words are used in the book. Choose one of the vocabulary activity sheets (pages 15 or 16) for students to complete as they read this section. Monitor students as they work to ensure the definitions they have found are accurate and relate to the text. Finally, discuss these important vocabulary words with students. If you think these words or other words in the section warrant more time devoted to them, there are suggestions in the introduction for other vocabulary activities (page 5).

Word	Definition	Sentence about Text
meticulously (ch. 1)	taking or showing extreme care about minute details; precise; thorough	Little Man **meticulously** straightens the collar on his shirt.
raucous (ch. 1)	harsh and loud, raspy	The **raucous** voices from the mouths of the boys show their anger at the passing bus.
sharecropping (ch. 1)	a system of farming developed in the South after the Civil War where former slaves would share and take care of land for its owner	The Logan family had been **sharecropping** with the plantation owner ever since the war ended.
tarpaulin (ch. 1)	a heavy waterproof covering, also known as a tarp	Cassie lifts the **tarpaulin** and counts over 30 classroom textbooks.
maverick (ch. 1)	a person who rebels to do their own thing	Mrs. Logan teaches her students a bit differently than others and is considered a **maverick**.
sinewy (ch. 2)	to have strong tendons in the body	Mama stands in the fields for hours due to her powerful and **sinewy** legs.
chiffonier (ch. 2)	a high chest with drawers and usually a mirror	Cassie places her clothes in the **chiffonier** that is near the front of the bedroom.
chrome (ch. 3)	a bright metallic trim	Mr. Granger drives his sleek **chrome**-covered car down the dusty road.
gully (ch. 3)	a small valley worn away by running water	The children dig furiously near the side of the road until they create a **gully** for the water.
caravan (ch. 3)	a group of travelers	A **caravan** of vehicles screeches to a halt right in front of the Logan house in the middle of the night.

Name _____

Date _____

Understanding Vocabulary Words

Directions: The following words are found in this section of the book. Use context clues and reference materials to determine an accurate definition for each word.

Word	Definition
meticulously (ch. 1)	
raucous (ch. 1)	
sharecropping (ch. 1)	
tarpaulin (ch. 1)	
maverick (ch. 1)	
sinewy (ch. 2)	
chiffonier (ch. 2)	
chrome (ch. 3)	
gully (ch. 3)	
caravan (ch. 3)	

Name _____

Date _____

During-Reading Vocabulary Activity

Directions: As you read these chapters, record at least eight important words on the lines below. Try to find interesting, difficult, intriguing, special, or funny words. Your words can be long or short. They can be hard or easy to spell. After each word, use context clues in the text and reference materials to define the word.

- _____
- _____
- _____
- _____
- _____
- _____
- _____
- _____
- _____
- _____

Directions: Respond to the following questions about these words in this section.

1. In what way does Little Man act like a **maverick**?

_____

_____

2. How do the Logans create the **gully** in the middle of the road?

_____

_____

Analyzing the Literature

Provided below are discussion questions you can use in small groups, with the whole class, or for written assignments. Each question is given at two levels so you can choose the right question for each group of students. Activity sheets with these questions are provided (pages 18–19) if you want students to write their responses. For each question, a few key discussion points are provided for your reference.

Story Element	■ Level 1	▲ Level 2	Key Discussion Points
Character	Why does Little Man refuse to take his textbook from Miss Crocker?	Explain why Cassie and her brother react the way they do when they receive their textbooks.	Little Man stomps on and refuses to take the book because of a racial term on the inside cover. Race plays an important role throughout the story. Understanding the symbolism behind many of the prejudiced remarks and actions can help students relate to the main characters in the story.
Setting	Describe the children's journey to school each morning. What is their school like?	What makes the walk to school each day difficult for the children? What makes the walk worth the effort for them?	Students have to walk over an hour to get to a very old and crumbling schoolhouse. The teachers stress the gift of education bestowed to students and downplay the lack of materials and funds provided compared to white schools.
Plot	Describe the plan to get revenge on the bus and what happens to the bus.	Why do the Logans decide to get revenge on the bus that passes them every morning?	Stacey, Cassie, and the little boys have grown tired of the humiliation from the white students and the bus driver who drive past every day. They decide to dig a gully aided by the driving rain that will cause the bus to get stuck and break down.

Name _____

Date _____

■ Analyzing the Literature

Directions: Think about the section you have just read. Read each question and state your response with textual evidence.

1. Why does Little Man refuse to take his textbook from Miss Crocker?

_____

_____

_____

_____

_____

_____

2. Describe the children's journey to school each morning. What is their school like?

_____

_____

_____

_____

_____

3. Describe the plan to get revenge on the bus and what happens to the bus.

_____

_____

_____

_____

_____

Name _____

Date _____

▲ Analyzing the Literature

Directions: Think about the section you have just read. Read each question and state your response with textual evidence.

1. Explain why Cassie and her brother react the way they do when they receive their textbooks.

_____

_____

_____

_____

_____

2. What makes the walk to school each day difficult for the children? What makes the walk worth the effort for them?

_____

_____

_____

_____

_____

3. Why do the Logans decide to get revenge on the bus that passes them every morning?

_____

_____

_____

_____

_____

Name _____

Date _____

Reader Response

Directions: Choose one of the following prompts about this section to answer. Be sure you include a topic sentence in your response, use textual evidence to support your opinion, and provide a strong conclusion that summarizes your opinion.

Writing Prompts

- **Narrative Piece**—In this section, the Logan children face many problems due to their race. Write about a time that you faced a problem because of your race or gender.
- **Opinion/Argument Piece**—Explain the problem with the textbooks and offer Cassie and Mrs. Logan advice on how to solve the problem.

_____

_____

_____

_____

_____

_____

_____

_____

_____

_____

_____

_____

_____

_____

Name _____

Date _____

Close Reading the Literature

Directions: Closely reread the section in chapter 1 when Miss Crocker confronts Mrs. Logan about Cassie and Little Man's actions at school. Start with, "Mama's classroom was in the back . . . ." Continue until the end of the chapter. Read each question and then revisit the text to find the evidence that supports your answer.

1. Based on the text, what punishment does Miss Crocker tell Mama she gave the children?

   _____

   _____

   _____

   _____

2. How is Mama's reaction to the news about her children different from what Miss Crocker expected?

   _____

   _____

   _____

3. Describe what Mama does with Little Man's and Cassie's classroom books and explain why she decides to do it.

   _____

   _____

   _____

   _____

4. Give evidence from the text to support Cassie's belief that Mama "understood."

   _____

   _____

   _____

   _____

Name _____

Date _____

Making Connections—Through the Years

Directions: Refer to the chart that is on the inside front cover of the school's textbooks to answer the following questions.

Question	Answer
How many years ago was the textbook new?	
Cassie is 9 years old in 1933. What condition was the textbook in the year she was born?	
Mildred Taylor was born in 1943. How old would this book have been in the year that she went to kindergarten? (She would have been 5.)	
The Civil War started in 1861 and lasted for four years. How many years after the war ended did Cassie get this book?	
Schools in Mississippi were desegregated in 1970. How old would Cassie have been by that point?	

© Shell Education

Creating with the Story Elements

Directions: Thinking about the story elements of character, setting, and plot in a novel is very important to understanding what is happening and why. Complete **one** of the following activities about what you've read so far. Be creative and have fun!

Characters

Select one of the children from the book. Write his or her name vertically on a piece of paper. Try to think of a phrase or sentence that begins with each letter of that character's name. The phrases or sentences should be about the character's personality or some aspect of his or her life.

Setting

Use books or the Internet to research facts about the state of Mississippi. Create a poster for the state on a piece of construction paper. Include written and drawn facts about the state that you find interesting. Some ideas might include the state flag, important cities, climate, and the state bird.

Plot

Create a board game about the children traveling to school. Create spaces on the board that are relevant to the actual journey the children make. Include obstacles and shortcuts that are mentioned in the book. You can also add new obstacles that you think might have been part of their journey.

Vocabulary Overview

Ten key words from this section are provided below with definitions and sentences about how the words are used in the book. Choose one of the vocabulary activity sheets (pages 25 or 26) for students to complete as they read this section. Monitor students as they work to ensure the definitions they have found are accurate and relate to the text. Finally, discuss these important vocabulary words with students. If you think these words or other words in the section warrant more time devoted to them, there are suggestions in the introduction for other vocabulary activities (page 5).

Word	Definition	Sentence about Text
churn (ch. 4)	to stir to make cream into butter	Cassie has to **churn** the butter for the family.
aloof (ch. 4)	distant, cold	Cassie watches the boys fighting with an **aloof** expression, afraid to move closer.
engrossed (ch. 4)	occupied completely with attention	The children are so **engrossed** in the fight that they do not notice Mr. Morrison pull up in the wagon.
nauseous (ch. 4)	to feel sick in the stomach	Stacey feels **nauseous** inside knowing the trouble that waits once he returns home.
fathom (ch. 4)	to understand	Mama cannot **fathom** why the children disobey her and go to the Wallace store.
patronize (ch. 4)	giving business to a company	The Logan family is looking for another store to **patronize** in Strawberry.
proprietor (ch. 4)	the owner of a business	The **proprietor** of the supply store ignores T.J. when a white person interrupts and asks to be helped.
bunion (ch. 5)	a swelling of the big toe	After walking all day, Mama begins to develop a **bunion** on her left foot.
veranda (ch. 5)	an open porch on the outside of a building	Many supplies are stacked in boxes and placed for sale on the **veranda**.
retaliated (ch. 5)	to get back at someone for wrongdoing	Cassie knows it is not in her best interest to **retaliate** when Lillian Jean makes rude comments to her.

Name _____

Date _____

Understanding Vocabulary Words

Directions: The following words are found in this section of the book. Use context clues and reference materials to determine an accurate definition for each word.

Word	Definition
churn (ch. 4)	
aloof (ch. 4)	
engrossed (ch. 4)	
nauseous (ch. 4)	
fathom (ch. 4)	
patronize (ch. 4)	
proprietor (ch. 4)	
bunion (ch. 5)	
veranda (ch. 5)	
retaliated (ch. 5)	

Name _____

Date _____

During-Reading Vocabulary Activity

Directions: As you read these chapters, record at least eight important words on the lines below. Try to find interesting, difficult, intriguing, special, or funny words. Your words can be long or short. They can be hard or easy to spell. After each word, use context clues in the text and reference materials to define the word.

- _____
- _____
- _____
- _____
- _____
- _____
- _____
- _____
- _____
- _____

Directions: Respond to the following questions about these words in this section.

1. Why is the **proprietor** of the Barnett mercantile store always interrupting T.J.'s supply order?

   _____

   _____

2. How does Stacey **retaliate** once he takes a punishment that was meant for T.J?

   _____

   _____

Analyzing the Literature

Provided below are discussion questions you can use in small groups, with the whole class, or for written assignments. Each question is given at two levels so you can choose the right question for each group of students. Activity sheets with these questions are provided (pages 28–29) if you want students to write their responses. For each question, a few key discussion points are provided for your reference.

Story Element	■ Level 1	▲ Level 2	Key Discussion Points
Character	What do you think causes Cassie to break the dish at the beginning of chapter 4?	Why does Big Ma think something is wrong with Cassie at the beginning of chapter 4?	Cassie is definitely showing signs of concern and nervousness at the events that have already occurred. Her grandmother has begun to get suspicious as to how much Cassie actually knows.
Plot	What does T.J. plan to do at school to help him succeed on his test?	Give an explanation as to why Stacey angrily runs after T.J. once school lets out.	T.J. brings notes that help him cheat on the test at school. Stacey takes the notes to prevent T.J. from cheating, but Mama catches Stacey. After he is punished, he goes after T.J. and fights him in front of the Wallace store.
Plot	Why does Mama bring the children to visit the Berry family?	What lesson do the children learn by visiting the Berry house?	To show the children the reason they are forbidden to go near the store owned by the Wallace family, Mama brings them to the Berry home. Mr. Berry was burned and disfigured by a fire set intentionally by members of the Wallace family.
Plot	How does Cassie end up on the ground after the confrontation with Lillian Jean?	Why is saying sorry to Lillian Jean one of the cruelest and hardest things Cassie has ever had to say?	After leaving the supply store in anger, Cassie accidently bumps into Lillian Jean. Lillian Jean's angry father pushes Cassie down to show his displeasure at what has taken place. After pleading her case, Big Ma forces Cassie to apologize to Lillian Jean.

Name _____

Date _____

Analyzing the Literature

Directions: Think about the section you have just read. Read each question and state your response with textual evidence.

1. What do you think causes Cassie to break the dish at the beginning of chapter 4?

   _____

   _____

   _____

   _____

2. What does T.J. plan to do at school to help him succeed on his test?

   _____

   _____

   _____

   _____

3. Why does Mama bring the children to visit the Berry family?

   _____

   _____

   _____

   _____

4. How does Cassie end up on the ground after the confrontation with Lillian Jean?

   _____

   _____

   _____

Name _____

Date _____

▲ Analyzing the Literature

Directions: Think about the section you have just read. Read each question and state your response with textual evidence.

1. Why does Big Ma think something is wrong with Cassie at the beginning of chapter 4?

   _____

   _____

   _____

2. Give an explanation as to why Stacey angrily runs after T.J. once school lets out.

   _____

   _____

   _____

3. What lesson do the children learn by visiting the Berry house?

   _____

   _____

   _____

4. Why is saying sorry to Lillian Jean one of the cruelest and hardest things Cassie has ever had to say?

   _____

   _____

   _____

   _____

Name _____

Date _____

Reader Response

Directions: Choose one of the following prompts about this section to answer. Be sure you include a topic sentence in your response, use textual evidence to support your opinion, and provide a strong conclusion that summarizes your opinion.

Writing Prompts

- **Narrative Piece**—Tell about a time when people you know did something that their parents forbade them to do. Explain their reasons for breaking the rules.
- **Informative/Explanatory Piece**—What do you learn about Cassie Logan in this section that you think will be important later in the novel?

_____

_____

_____

_____

_____

_____

_____

_____

_____

_____

_____

_____

_____

_____

Name _____

Date _____

Close Reading the Literature

Directions: Closely reread the section toward the end of chapter 4 that starts with, "Despite our every effort to persuade Stacey otherwise . . ." and continue until, "That's why I don't want you to ever go to their store again—for any reason. You understand?" Read each question and then revisit the text to find the evidence that supports your answer.

1. Use the text to describe what the children see the first time they notice Mr. Berry.

   _____

   _____

   _____

   _____

2. Based on the text, explain what the Wallaces did to Mr. Berry and his nephews.

   _____

   _____

   _____

   _____

3. Based on the events in the story, why did Mama bring the children to the Berrys for a visit?

   _____

   _____

   _____

   _____

4. Using what you know about the Logan children, how do you think this visit will affect them?

   _____

   _____

   _____

   _____

Name _____

Date _____

Making Connections–Growing Seeds

The Logan family grows most of the food they need to survive. It takes years for farmers to learn how to produce the best crops. Follow the steps below to figure out what works best for your seeds. You will plant some seeds and follow their growth.

Materials

- one type of seed (3 seeds)
- potting soil
- containers to hold soil and seeds (egg cartons or small cups work well)
- water
- distilled water
- salt

Procedures

1. Label the containers with the following titles: plain water, salt water, and distilled water.
2. Fill three containers about two-thirds full of soil.
3. Place one seed in each container.
4. Water each container with the right type of water. (You'll have to mix the salt into the water before using it.)
5. Place the containers somewhere warm with sunlight.
6. Keep the soil moist by watering (with the correct water) every couple of days. Water the plants with the same amount of water each time.

Response

Recreate the following chart and record your observations.

	Plain Water	Distilled Water	Salt Water
Growth after 1 week			
Growth after 2 weeks			
Growth after 3 weeks			
and so on . . .			

Name _____

Date _____

Creating with the Story Elements

Directions: Thinking about the story elements of character, setting, and plot in a novel is very important to understanding what is happening and why. Complete **one** of the following activities about what you've read so far. Be creative and have fun!

Characters

Pretend T.J. and Stacey have to go to court and explain their sides of the story about the fight they had. Write dialogue between Stacey, T.J., and the judge. Have each boy give reasons that show justification as to why he did what he did.

Setting

Many businesses did not welcome African Americans during the time following the Civil War. Pretend that you are the owner of a new supply store during this time. Design a store advertisement that invites people of all races to shop at your store. You want to be competitive, but you also want to be fair to all people. Now is your chance to invite them in with a one-page poster advertising your store.

Plot

Create two comic strips. On the first comic strip, write and draw the real altercation that takes place between Cassie and Lillian Jean at the end of chapter 5. On the second comic strip, write and draw what could have happened if both characters had made better decisions in their interaction with one other.

Vocabulary Overview

Ten key words from this section are provided below with definitions and sentences about how the words are used in the book. Choose one of the vocabulary activity sheets (pages 35 or 36) for students to complete as they read this section. Monitor students as they work to ensure the definitions they have found are accurate and relate to the text. Finally, discuss these important vocabulary words with students. If you think these words or other words in the section warrant more time devoted to them, there are suggestions in the introduction for other vocabulary activities (page 5).

Word	Definition	Sentence about Text
sulked (ch. 6)	to be silent because of a wrong done; usually for sympathy	Cassie **sulks** in the back of the wagon after her confrontation with Lillian Jean.
expound (ch. 6)	to explain	Uncle Hammer **expounds** on his story about the new car that is parked outside the house.
awestruck (ch. 6)	overcome with admiration	The children are **awestruck** when Uncle Hammer shows them the inside of his shiny, new car.
ominously (ch. 6)	a feeling of harm or evil occurring in the future	Little Man **ominously** predicts that Uncle Hammer and Mr. Simms will confront each other sooner or later.
obedience (ch. 6)	to obey	The children know that Mama and Pa expect **obedience** from them.
chignon (ch. 6)	a large knot or roll of hair worn on the back of the neck	Mama helps place a **chignon** on Cassie's head as they dress for church.
preacher (ch. 7)	a person who delivers material related to a type of religion	The **preacher** stands in front of all of the church members and delivers his message.
interminable (ch. 7)	unending	The last day of school before the Christmas holiday seems to take an **interminable** amount of time.
flounce (ch. 7)	to move the body in exaggerated movements	With a smirk on her face, Lillian Jean **flounces** past Cassie on her way to school.
boycott (ch. 7)	to refuse to buy or use	Mama tries to get community members to **boycott** shopping at the Wallace store.

Name _____

Date _____

Understanding Vocabulary Words

Directions: The following words are in this section of the book. Use context clues and reference materials to determine an accurate definition for each word.

Word	Definition
sulked (ch. 6)	
expound (ch. 6)	
awestruck (ch. 6)	
ominously (ch. 6)	
obedience (ch. 6)	
chignon (ch. 6)	
preacher (ch. 7)	
interminable (ch. 7)	
flounce (ch. 7)	
boycott (ch. 7)	

Name _____

Date _____

During-Reading Vocabulary Activity

Directions: As you read these chapters, record at least eight important words on the lines below. Try to find interesting, difficult, intriguing, special, or funny words. Your words can be long or short. They can be hard or easy to spell. After each word, use context clues in the text and reference materials to define the word.

- _____

- _____

- _____

- _____

- _____

- _____

- _____

- _____

- _____

- _____

Directions: Now, organize your words. Rewrite each of your words on a sticky note. Work as a group to create a bar graph of your words. You should stack any words that are the same on top of one another. Different words appear in different columns. Finally, discuss with your teacher why certain words were chosen more often than other words.

Analyzing the Literature

Provided below are discussion questions you can use in small groups, with the whole class, or for written assignments. Each question is given at two levels so you can choose the right question for each group of students. Activity sheets with these questions are provided (pages 38–39) if you want students to write their responses. For each question, a few key discussion points are provided for your reference.

Story Element	■ Level 1	▲ Level 2	Key Discussion Points
Character	What is Uncle Hammer's reaction when he hears the news about Cassie and Lillian Jean?	How do the views of Big Ma and Uncle Hammer differ when discussing the incident about Lillian Jean?	Uncle Hammer is in disbelief when he hears what happened to Cassie. When Big Ma downplays the incident noting that Cassie did not get hurt, Uncle Hammer objects and points out the *hurt* Cassie is feeling emotionally.
Setting	Name some of the foods that fill the Logan household on Christmas Day.	Describe the sights, smells, and sounds at the Logan house on Christmas Day.	The Logan family provides a huge feast for the family on Christmas. A variety of food is provided and the house is decorated for the occasion.
Plot	How do the Wallace children mistake Uncle Hammer for Mr. Granger?	Explain why you think Uncle Hammer continues to pretend to be Mr. Granger when they encounter the Wallace children.	Uncle Hammer is mistaken for Mr. Granger due to the fact that they are dressed similarly and drive the same type of car. Once the Wallace children acknowledge Uncle Hammer as Mr. Granger, he continues to play along by nodding back at the children.
Plot	What is the purpose of Mr. Granger's visit to the Logan family?	How do you know that Uncle Hammer and Papa are not afraid of the threats made by Mr. Granger?	Mr. Granger is aware of the Logan family's attempt to get others to boycott certain stores and warns them about doing so. Uncle Hammer and Papa stand firm and are not intimidated by his words.

Name _____

Date _____

Analyzing the Literature

Directions: Think about the section you have just read. Read each question and state your response with textual evidence.

1. What is Uncle Hammer's reaction when he hears the news about Cassie and Lillian Jean?

_____

_____

_____

_____

2. Name some of the foods that fill the Logan household on Christmas Day.

_____

_____

_____

_____

3. How do the Wallace children mistake Uncle Hammer for Mr. Granger?

_____

_____

_____

_____

4. What is the purpose of Mr. Granger's visit to the Logan family?

_____

_____

_____

_____

Name _____

Date _____

▲ Analyzing the Literature

Directions: Think about the section you have just read. Read each question and state your response with textual evidence.

1. How do the views of Big Ma and Uncle Hammer differ when discussing the incident about Lillian Jean?

   _____

   _____

   _____

   _____

2. Describe the sights, smells, and sounds at the Logan house on Christmas Day.

   _____

   _____

   _____

3. Explain why you think Uncle Hammer continues to pretend to be Mr. Granger when they encounter the Wallace children.

   _____

   _____

   _____

   _____

4. How do you know that Uncle Hammer and Papa are not afraid of the threats made by Mr. Granger?

   _____

   _____

   _____

   _____

Name _____

Date _____

Reader Response

Directions: Choose one of the following prompts about this section to answer. Be sure you include a topic sentence in your response, use textual evidence to support your opinion, and provide a strong conclusion that summarizes your opinion.

Writing Prompts

- **Opinion/Argument Piece**—Describe why you would or would not like to have lived in the time and place of this story.
- **Narrative Piece**—Imagine how the conversation between Mr. Granger and the Logans would have gone if they were all the same race. Rewrite the scene.

_____

_____

_____

_____

_____

_____

_____

_____

_____

_____

_____

_____

_____

_____

_____

Name _____

Date _____

Close Reading the Literature

Directions: Closely reread the section toward the end of chapter 7 where Mr. Granger arrives at the Logan farm. Start with, "In the days that followed . . ." and continue until the end of the chapter. Read each question and then revisit the text to find the evidence that supports your answer.

1. Use the book to tell what Mr. Granger has heard from community members about the Logans' plan for shopping.

_____

_____

_____

_____

2. Describe what Mr. Granger is talking about when Uncle Hammer responds by saying, "Ain't gonna lose it."

_____

_____

_____

_____

3. For what reasons does Mr. Granger turn his attention away from Papa and Uncle Hammer and start talking to Mama?

_____

_____

_____

_____

4. Use the text to describe the end of the conversation between Papa and Mr. Granger. What does each promise to do?

_____

_____

_____

_____

Name _____

Date _____

Making Connections–Character Dialect

Many people have special ways of speaking because of where they have grown up. Even though people may all be speaking English, there are different ways of saying the same thing. For example, some people use the phrase "standing in line," while other people say "standing on line" when referring to standing and waiting for something. In this book, Cassie and her family use a dialect from their region and time. They use words like "wanna" for "want to," "I s'pose so" for the phrase "I suppose so," as well as the word "ain't" instead of "am not."

Directions: Create a dialect glossary for this book. Search the book for conversations between the characters. Make a list of words or phrases that provide examples of the Logan family's dialect. Write these words in the chart below and indicate what you think each means based on context clues.

Person Speaking	Dialect Words	Explanation

Name _____

Date _____

Creating with the Story Elements

Directions: Thinking about the story elements of character, setting, and plot in a novel is very important to understanding what is happening and why. Complete **one** of the following activities about what you've read so far. Be creative and have fun!

Characters

Draw a picture showing some of the gifts the children receive for Christmas. Include Uncle Hammer's gift to Stacey and Jeremy Simms's gift to the whole family. Label each of the gifts.

Setting

Compare and contrast the setting of your family's holiday meals with the Logan family's meal. Create a Venn diagram that shows the similarities and differences.

Plot

Imagine you are Stacey and you have just received a brand new coat from Uncle Hammer. Although you are appreciative of the coat, you do not want to wear it because of the way others have made fun of you. Write a letter to Uncle Hammer giving him thanks but also figure out a way to share your reasons for why you don't want to keep the jacket.

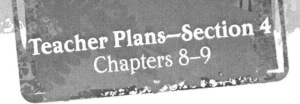

Vocabulary Overview

Ten key words from this section are provided below with definitions and sentences about how the words are used in the book. Choose one of the vocabulary activity sheets (pages 45 or 46) for students to complete as they read this section. Monitor students as they work to ensure the definitions they have found are accurate and relate to the text. Finally, discuss these important vocabulary words with students. If you think these words or other words in the section warrant more time devoted to them, there are suggestions in the introduction for other vocabulary activities (page 5).

Word	Definition	Descriptive Sentence
feigned (ch. 8)	to make believe	T.J. **feigns** an apology once Cassie yells at him for making comments about Mama.
examination (ch. 8)	a test	Cassie knows her **examination** is in two short weeks and wants to begin studying immediately.
sauntered (ch. 8)	to walk in a casual manner	Lillian Jean **saunters** down the crosswalk on her way into the school building.
tidbit (ch. 8)	a small piece of news or gossip	Cassie hears many different **tidbits** from Lillian Jean that she is supposed to keep secret.
glade (ch. 8)	an open space in a forest	Cassie leads Lillian Jean to the **glade** to give her a special surprise.
pasture (ch. 8)	an area covered in grass used to feed livestock	Papa and Cassie take a stroll across the **pasture** on their way to feed the animals.
indefinitely (ch. 9)	unlimited	The long school day seems to linger **indefinitely** during the morning hours.
pneumonia (ch. 9)	illness caused by bacteria in the lungs	Mama is afraid that Papa might catch **pneumonia** after being out in the cold rain for so long.
skittish (ch. 9)	shy, uncertain	Stacey tries to keep the **skittish** mule calm, while Papa fixes the wheel.
mortgage (ch. 9)	Agreement where one borrows money to buy property and agrees to pay it back	Mama is worried that the family will not be able to afford the **mortgage** for much longer.

Name _____

Date _____

Understanding Vocabulary Words

Directions: The following words are in this section of the book. Use context clues and reference materials to determine an accurate definition for each word.

Word	Definition
feigned (ch. 8)	
examination (ch. 8)	
sauntered (ch. 8)	
tidbit (ch. 8)	
glade (ch. 8)	
pasture (ch. 8)	
indefinitely (ch. 9)	
pneumonia (ch. 9)	
skittish (ch. 9)	
mortgage (ch. 9)	

Name _____

Date _____

During-Reading Vocabulary Activity

Directions: As you read these chapters, record at least eight important words on the lines below. Try to find interesting, difficult, intriguing, special, or funny words. Your words can be long or short. They can be hard or easy to spell. After each word, use context clues in the text and reference materials to define the word.

- _____
- _____
- _____
- _____
- _____
- _____
- _____
- _____
- _____
- _____

Directions: Respond to the following questions about these words in this section.

1. What is the real reason Cassie asks Lillian Jean to go to the **glade**?

   _____

   _____

2. How does T.J. perform on his **examinations** during the last few weeks of school?

   _____

   _____

Analyzing the Literature

Provided below are discussion questions you can use in small groups, with the whole class, or for written assignments. Each question is given at two levels so you can choose the right question for each group of students. Activity sheets with these questions are provided (pages 48–49) if you want students to write their responses. For each question, a few key discussion points are provided for your reference.

Story Element	■ Level 1	▲ Level 2	Key Discussion Points
Character	How does Cassie get revenge for all the mean things Lillian Jean has done?	Explain how Cassie gains the trust of Lillian Jean.	Cassie befriends Lillian Jean and pretends to enjoy doing whatever Lillian Jean asks. Lillian Jean confides in Cassie during this time, sharing many of her secrets. After about a month Cassie threatens and hurts Lillian Jean and tells her the whole thing was a setup.
Plot	What does T.J. tell the Wallace family that causes the Board of Education to attend and watch one of Mama's lessons in school?	Give details as to why Mr. Granger fires Mrs. Logan.	After failing his test, T.J. ends up telling members of the Wallace family that Mrs. Logan is changing the material that she is teaching. Mr. Granger uses this as an excuse to fire her, even though the real reason is because of her family's boycott of the store owned by the Wallaces.
Setting	Why is the Logan family traveling all the way to Vicksburg to do their shopping?	Give reasons why taking a day's trip to Vicksburg to shop is a better option for the Logans than shopping at the stores near their own farm.	To protest the treatment many families are receiving from the Wallaces, the Logan family tries to start a boycott of their store. They are traveling to a much farther store in Vicksburg and are encouraging others to do the same.
Plot	What happens to Papa, Stacey, and Mr. Morrison on their way back from Vicksburg?	Use the text to explain what happens to Papa as he tries to fix the wheel on the wagon.	On the way back from Vicksburg, some men ambush Papa, Stacey, and Mr. Morrison. The men shoot Papa, and his leg is crushed under the wagon wheel that he is trying to fix.

Name _____

Date _____

Analyzing the Literature

Directions: Think about the section you have just read. Read each question and state your response with textual evidence.

1. How does Cassie get revenge for all the mean things Lillian Jean has done?

   _____

   _____

   _____

   _____

2. What does T.J. tell the Wallace family that causes the Board of Education to attend and watch one of Mama's lessons in school?

   _____

   _____

   _____

   _____

3. Why is the Logan family traveling all the way to Vicksburg to do their shopping?

   _____

   _____

   _____

   _____

4. What happens to Papa, Stacey, and Mr. Morrison on their way back from Vicksburg?

   _____

   _____

   _____

Name _____

Date _____

▲ Analyzing the Literature

Directions: Think about the section you have just read. Read each question and state your response with textual evidence.

1. Explain how Cassie gains the trust of Lillian Jean.

_____

_____

_____

_____

2. Give details as to why Mr. Granger fires Mrs. Logan.

_____

_____

_____

_____

3. Give reasons why taking a day's trip to Vicksburg to shop is a better option for the Logans than shopping at the stores near their own farm.

_____

_____

_____

_____

4. Use the text to explain what happens to Papa as he tries to fix the wheel on the wagon.

_____

_____

_____

_____

Name _____

Date _____

Reader Response

Directions: Choose one of the following prompts about this section to answer. Be sure you include a topic sentence in your response, use textual evidence to support your opinion, and provide a strong conclusion that summarizes your opinion.

Writing Prompts

- **Informative/Explanatory Piece**—Compare and contrast characters in this book with people in your life. Describe how they are the same and different.
- **Opinion/Argument Piece**—Argue for or against this statement: *It is fair for the Board of Education members to fire Mrs. Logan.*

_____

_____

_____

_____

_____

_____

_____

_____

_____

_____

_____

_____

_____

_____

_____

_____

Name _____

Date _____

Close Reading the Literature

Directions: Closely reread the section at the end of chapter 9 where Papa, Stacey, and Mr. Morrison return from Vicksburg. Start with, "Out of the darkness a round light appeared, moving slowly across the drive . . ." Continue until the end of the chapter. Read each question and then revisit the text to find the evidence that supports your answer.

1. Use the text to give details about the injuries Papa receives on his way home from Vicksburg.

   _____

   _____

   _____

   _____

2. What text evidence helps the readers understand why Stacey blames himself for Papa's broken leg?

   _____

   _____

   _____

   _____

3. What evidence from the book lets the reader know how strong Mr. Morrison is?

   _____

   _____

   _____

   _____

4. Based on the events from this part of the story, what do you think the Logans will do next?

   _____

   _____

   _____

Name _____

Date _____

Making Connections–Boycott!

One of the major plot points in this book is the boycott of the Wallace Store by the Logan family and other members of the community. This was in response to all the wrongdoings caused by the Wallace family towards African Americans. During this time many African Americans began to stand up for themselves and this led to a movement known as the Civil Rights Movement. You have, no doubt, heard of many heroic figures such as Martin Luther King, Jr. and Rosa Parks, who worked for equality and stood up for what was right.

One of the more peaceful ways to protest acts of racial discrimination and prejudice is to organize and participate in a boycott. During a boycott, many civil rights followers would not shop or give money to businesses that did not treat people equally. Participants often carried signs and made simple chants or rhymes to voice their displeasure.

Directions: Pretend that you live at the time of the Logans. You want to help them organize their boycott of the Wallace Store. Complete **two** of these activities.

1. Create a sign that you could use to boycott the Wallace Store.

2. Create a chant or rhyme that participants could say while holding these signs. (Make sure your words are appropriate.)

3. Write a one-paragraph speech that a leader of the group could read out loud to all the participants of the boycott.

Name _____

Date _____

Creating with the Story Elements

Directions: Thinking about the story elements of character, setting, and plot in a novel is very important to understanding what is happening and why. Complete **one** of the following activities about what you've read so far. Be creative and have fun!

Characters

Write a list of questions that you might ask Lillian Jean in an interview. Think about how she treats Cassie when she is first introduced, but try to also keep in mind how she confides in Cassie about her life as you are developing your questions.

Setting

Draw a map from the Logan farm to Vicksburg. Include obstacles and items from the story that the family members may have come across on this journey.

Plot

Write the next chapter of the story. Now that Papa is home and Stacey has given the details as to what happened in Vicksburg, write what you think is going to happen next in the story. What do you think will happen to Papa? What will happen to the men who injured Papa?

Vocabulary Overview

Ten key words from this section are provided below with definitions and sentences about how the words are used in the book. Choose one of the vocabulary activity sheets (pages 55 or 56) for students to complete as they read this section. Monitor students as they work to ensure the definitions they have found are accurate and relate to the text. Finally, discuss these important vocabulary words with students. If you think these words or other words in the section warrant more time devoted to them, there are suggestions in the introduction for other vocabulary activities (page 5).

Word	Definition	Sentence about Text
ledger (ch. 10)	a book kept with financial numbers	Mama leaves her **ledger** on the table near the front door.
ginned (ch. 10)	to clear and clean cotton with a machine	Papa **gins** five acres of cotton from the field behind the house.
lethargic (ch. 10)	sluggish	During the hot, humid, summer, the children look **lethargic** as they cross through the fields.
revival (ch. 10)	a gathering to renew faith in a religion	Cassie is excited to participate in the **revival** with other members of the church.
condescending (ch. 10)	to act graciously towards others regarded as being at a lower level	Melvin gives a **condescending** smile when T.J. asks him about the pistol.
en masse (ch. 11)	together in a group	Members of the community walk **en masse** toward the cotton-filled plantation.
mercantile (ch. 11)	to trade	T.J. and his new friends break into the **mercantile** store and steal a pistol.
akimbo (ch. 11)	a hand on the hip and elbow bent outward	The man, who has one arm resting **akimbo** to his side, uses the other to knock on the door.
singe (ch. 12)	to burn, scorch	The residents watch hopelessly as the cotton plants **singe** to the ground.
adamant (ch. 12)	inflexible and without compromise	Mama is **adamant** when she tells Cassie to stay in the house.

Understanding Vocabulary Words

Directions: The following words are in this section of the book. Use context clues and reference materials to determine an accurate definition for each word.

Word	Definition
ledger (ch. 10)	
ginned (ch. 10)	
lethargic (ch. 10)	
revival (ch. 10)	
condescending (ch. 10)	
en masse (ch. 11)	
mercantile (ch. 11)	
akimbo (ch. 11)	
singe (ch. 12)	
adamant (ch. 12)	

Name _____

Date _____

During-Reading Vocabulary Activity

Directions: As you read these chapters, choose five important words from the story. Use these words to complete the word flow chart below. On each arrow, write a word. In each box, explain how the connected pair of words relates to each other. An example for the words *ginned* and *mercantile* has been done for you.

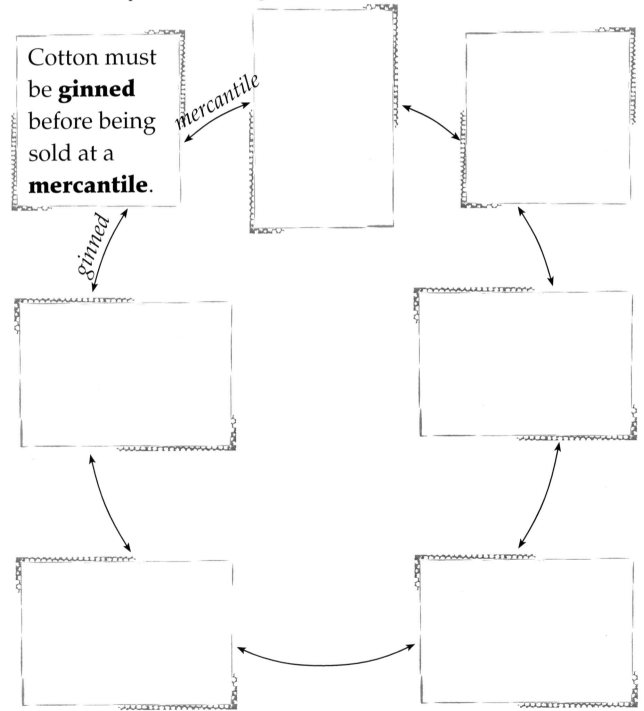

Cotton must be **ginned** before being sold at a **mercantile**.

Analyzing the Literature

Provided below are discussion questions you can use in small groups, with the whole class, or for written assignments. Each question is given at two levels so you can choose the right question for each group of students. Activity sheets with these questions are provided (pages 58–59) if you want students to write their responses. For each question, a few key discussion points are provided for your reference.

Story Element	■ Level 1	▲ Level 2	Key Discussion Points
Plot	Why do Cassie and Mr. Morrison go to see Mr. Wiggins?	Explain how Mr. Morrison gets around Kaleb Wallace's truck, which blocks his own wagon's path.	Mr. Morrison wants to take a planter owned by Papa over to Mr. Wiggins's farm. An angry Kaleb Wallace blocks Mr. Morrison's path with his truck. Kaleb shouts insults for what Mr. Morrison did to members of the Wallace family. Mr. Morrison calmly lifts the truck on both ends to move it out of the way.
Character	How does the family get the money to help pay off the mortgage that is due?	Why do you think Uncle Hammer is willing to sell his car and give the money to Papa?	Mama and Papa are very worried about making a payment on their mortgage. Although they are reluctant to do so at first, they finally ask Uncle Hammer. Uncle Hammer sells his car to get the money. He does not want the family to lose the farm to the Grangers.
Plot	How does T.J. get the bruises on his chest?	Give reasons why Stacey and Cassie do not believe T.J.'s story when he first tells it.	T.J. sneaks into the Logan house and tells Stacey and Cassie he is trouble. He explains how he and the Wallace boys stole a pistol and hurt Mr. and Mrs. Barnett in the process. When T.J. threatens to confess everything, his two white "friends" beat him. Stacey and Cassie have a hard time believing T.J. after all they have been through.
Setting	How does Big Ma think the fire that burned much of their farm started?	Explain why Mr. Granger orders the men to leave T.J. alone and head to the forest.	When Big Ma sees the smoke on the farm, she suspects it was caused by a nearby lightning strike. When Mr. Granger realizes the fire is headed toward land he owns, he urges the residents to help put the fire out.

Name _____

Date _____

Analyzing the Literature

Directions: Think about the section you have just read. Read each question and state your response with textual evidence.

1. Why do Cassie and Mr. Morrison go to see Mr. Wiggins?

_____

_____

_____

_____

2. How does the family get the money to help pay off the mortgage that is due?

_____

_____

_____

_____

3. How does T.J. get the bruises on his chest?

_____

_____

_____

_____

4. How does Big Ma think the fire that burned much of their farm started?

_____

_____

_____

_____

Name _____

Date _____

▲ Analyzing the Literature

Directions: Think about the section you have just read. Read each question and state your response with textual evidence.

1. Explain how Mr. Morrison gets around Kaleb Wallace's truck, which blocks his own wagon's path.

_____

_____

_____

_____

2. Why do you think Uncle Hammer is willing to sell his car and give the money to Papa?

_____

_____

_____

3. Give reasons why Stacey and Cassie do not believe T.J.'s story when he first tells it.

_____

_____

_____

_____

4. Explain why Mr. Granger orders the men to leave T.J. alone and head to the forest.

_____

_____

_____

Name _____

Date _____

Reader Response

Directions: Choose one of the following prompts about this section to answer. Be sure you include a topic sentence in your response, use textual evidence to support your opinion, and provide a strong conclusion that summarizes your opinion.

Writing Prompts

- **Informative/Explanatory Piece**—Describe a personal quality of Cassie that you think would be a good characteristic to develop within yourself.
- **Narrative Piece**—Pick a scene in which you disagree with how a character handles a situation. Rewrite the scene how you think it should have happened.

_____

_____

_____

_____

_____

_____

_____

_____

_____

_____

_____

_____

_____

_____

_____

Name _____

Date _____

Close Reading the Literature

Directions: Closely reread the section in the middle of chapter 11 where Cassie, Stacey, Christopher John, and Little Man decide to take T.J. back to his house. Start with, "The thunder was creeping closer now, . . ." and continue until the sheriff is mentioned with, "Where's Hank?" Read each question and then revisit the text to find the evidence that supports your answer.

1. Describe what the children see coming closer as they turn to leave T.J.'s house.

    _____

    _____

    _____

2. Use text evidence to describe how the men get T.J's family outside.

    _____

    _____

    _____

3. Use the book to explain Kaleb Wallace's version about what happened at Mr. and Mrs. Barnett's store.

    _____

    _____

    _____

    _____

4. In what ways is it significant that Mr. Jamison arrives at the scene?

    _____

    _____

    _____

    _____

Name _____

Date _____

Making Connections—Report on Civil Rights

Roll of Thunder, Hear My Cry takes place during the 1930s. Even though it is a work of fiction, many of the places, historical figures, and plot points are true. Here is a list of some important events related to the time frame of this book:

- *Brown v. Board of Education* Supreme Court Case
- The Great Depression
- The Civil Rights Movement
- Martin Luther King Jr.'s "I Have a Dream" speech

Directions: Choose one of these events. Then, research the event using the questions below as a guide. Create a one-page report that summarizes what you learn.

1. What is the significance of the event?
2. Who are some of the people involved and what were their roles in the event?
3. Why is this event still important today?
4. How have things changed since this event occurred?

Name _____

Date _____

Creating with the Story Elements

Directions: Thinking about the story elements of character, setting, and plot in a novel is very important to understanding what is happening and why. Complete **one** of the following activities about what you've read so far. Be creative and have fun!

Characters

Cassie has been through a lot in this story. She goes through many different emotions. Think about two or three different emotions that Cassie experiences in the last section of the book. For each example, describe what she is feeling and draw what you visualize from the story.

Setting

The weather on the night of the climax of this story takes a turn for the worse. Lightning, thunder, and even heavy rain occur over the long evening and into early morning. Write a detailed weather report from midnight to 6:00 a.m. that includes some of the details from the book.

Plot

What do you think would have happened if someone saw Papa set fire to the fields? Write a new ending to this scenario and describe how the community would have reacted. What would happen to T.J.? The Logan family? Their farm?

Name _____

Date _____

Post-Reading Theme Thoughts

Directions: Read each of the statements in the first column. Choose a main character from *Roll of Thunder, Hear My Cry*. Think about that character's point of view. From that character's perspective, decide if the character would agree or disagree with the statements. Record the character's opinion by marking an *X* in Agree or Disagree for each statement. Explain your choices in the third column using text evidence.

Character I Chose: _____

Statement	Agree	Disagree	Explain Your Answer
You can always count on your family.			
Owning land is a symbol of independence.			
Sometimes you have to suffer to learn.			
It is wrong to treat people unfairly based on the color of their skin.			

Name _____

Date _____

Culminating Activity: Totally Not Fair!

There are many instances throughout this book where African Americans are treated differently than others. Although slavery was illegal in the United States during the 1930s, this did not mean that all white people treated African Americans as equals. Name calling, segregation, and violence are just some instances of hate that many African Americans endured during this time.

Directions: Think back to how the characters in *Roll of Thunder, Hear My Cry* go through their hardships. What are some examples of racism and prejudice experienced by the characters in this story? Try to list at least ten different examples from the book.

Character Affected	Description of Racism or Prejudice

Name _____

Date _____

Culminating Activity: Totally Not Fair! *(cont.)*

Directions: Now that your list of racist or prejudice treatment is finished, complete **one** of the culminating projects below:

1. Take one incident from your list and make it the title of a fictional movie about the time period. Create a movie poster that shows what might happen in the movie.

3. Select two or three situations from your list. Focus on the characters that are mistreating others. Create a mini "Wanted" poster for each guilty character in those situations. For each situation, draw his or her picture and describe what he or she did under the picture.

2. Write a letter to one of the characters you listed. Pretend you were there to witness the situation that occurred. Let the character know what you saw and then give him or her advice on how to respond. Try to give a suggestion for what he or she could do if this mistreatment ever happens again.

Name _____

Date _____

Comprehension Assessment

Directions: Circle the letter for the best response to each question.

1. Which of these sentences helps the reader understand the meaning of the word *gully* as it's used in the book?

    a. Cassie and the others write the word *gully* in the front of their schoolbooks.

    b. Little Man uses the shovel furiously to help dig a *gully* that the bus would soon cross.

    c. Cassie does not know the meaning of *gully*, so she asks Miss Crocker.

    d. Stacey answers Cassie's question with only two words, "the gully."

2. Which of the following best describes where a gully might be found based on your answer from number 1?

    e. inside a school

    f. on the side of a road

    g. on a sheet of paper

    h. at home

3. Which statement best expresses one of the themes of the book?

    a. If you don't have anything nice to say, don't say anything.

    b. People of a certain race deserve more than those from another race.

    c. In order to succeed, one must own land, save a lot of money, and have a family.

    d. It is wrong to treat people unfairly based on the color of their skin.

4. What detail from the book provides the best evidence for your answer to number 3?

    e. "Cheat notes! But how'd T.J. get cheat notes? Stacey got rid of them things this morning."

    f. "I'm a Southerner, born and bred, but that doesn't mean I approve of all that goes on here, and there are a lot of other white people who feel the same."

    g. "Ah, there's my Cassie girl!" Papa laughed, standing to catch me as I leapt into his arms.

    h. Stacey did not let him finish. Jumping up, he pulled T.J. up too and hit him squarely in the face.

Comprehension Assessment (cont.)

5. What is the main idea of the text below?

"In the afternoon when I awakened, or tomorrow or the next day, the boys and I would still be free to run the red road, to wander through the old forest and sprawl lazily on the banks of the pond. Come October, we would trudge to school as always, barefooted and grumbling, fighting the dust and the mud and the Jefferson Davis school bus. But T.J. never would again."

_____

6. What details from those below support your answer to #5?

    a. Cassie and Little Man would continue their education next fall.

    b. T.J. is upset whenever the Jefferson Davis bus passes by.

    c. Cassie is free to relax near the water and the trees.

    d. Cassie starts school in the middle of the summer.

7. What is the meaning of this section of the poem from the book?

    "Ole man comin'
    down the line
    Whip in hand to
    beat me down
    But I ain't
    gonna let him
    Turn me 'round"

_____

_____

_____

8. Which of the following characters from the story best symbolizes "the ole man" from the poem?

    e. Papa

    f. Uncle Hammer

    g. Kaleb Wallace

    h. Mr. Jameson

Response to Literature: Researching Reconstruction

Directions: Following the Civil War, many Southern states had cities and towns that had been destroyed due to the battles between the Confederate and Union armies. The time that followed was known as Reconstruction. Search the Internet and other resources for information about this time period and see how many of the following answers you can discover. Group ideas together and write a two- to three-page report explaining the ideas behind Reconstruction. This is just a sample list of questions to get you started. Any other pieces of information relevant to Reconstruction are welcome in your report.

Questions to consider:
- Why was this time known as Reconstruction?
- Where were some of the most impacted locations?
- What happened to Confederate money?
- How were African Americans affected?
- What is sharecropping, and why was it created?

Name _____

Date _____

Response to Literature Rubric

Directions: Use this rubric to evaluate student responses to the ideas about Reconstruction.

	Exceptional Writing	Quality Writing	Developing Writing
Focus and Organization	☐ States a clear opinion and elaborates well. Engages the reader from hook through the middle to the conclusion. Demonstrates clear understanding of the intended audience and purpose of the piece.	☐ Provides a clear and consistent opinion. Maintains a clear perspective and supports it through elaborating details. Makes the opinion clear in the opening hook and summarizes well in the conclusion.	☐ Provides an inconsistent point of view. Does not support the topic adequately or misses pertinent information. Provides lack of clarity in the beginning, middle, and conclusion.
Text Evidence	☐ Provides comprehensive and accurate support. Includes relevant and worthwhile text references.	☐ Provides limited support. Provides few supporting text references.	☐ Provides very limited support for the text. Provides no supporting text references.
Written Expression	☐ Uses descriptive and precise language with clarity and intention. Maintains a consistent voice and uses an appropriate tone that supports meaning. Uses multiple sentence types and transitions well between ideas.	☐ Uses a broad vocabulary. Maintains a consistent voice and supports a tone and feelings through language. Varies sentence length and word choices.	☐ Uses a limited and unvaried vocabulary. Provides an inconsistent or weak voice and tone. Provides little to no variation in sentence type and length.
Language Conventions	☐ Capitalizes, punctuates, and spells accurately. Demonstrates complete thoughts within sentences, with accurate subject-verb agreement. Uses paragraphs appropriately and with clear purpose.	☐ Capitalizes, punctuates, and spells accurately. Demonstrates complete thoughts within sentences and appropriate grammar. Paragraphs are properly divided and supported.	☐ Incorrectly capitalizes, punctuates, and spells. Uses fragmented or run-on sentences. Utilizes poor grammar overall. Paragraphs are poorly divided and developed.

The responses provided here are just examples of what students may answer. Many accurate responses are possible for the questions throughout this unit.

During-Reading Vocabulary Activity—Section 1: Chapters 1–3 (page 16)

1. Little Man behaves like a **maverick** when he is given his book at school. He realizes it is not the same as white students receive and proceeds to throw it on the floor and stomp on it.

2. The children create the **gully** after taking shovels from the tool shed at school. They use the shovels to dig holes in the middle of the road. The plan is to trap the bus that eventually passes.

Close Reading the Literature—Section 1: Chapters 1–3 (page 21)

1. Miss Crocker tells Mama that she whips Cassie and Little Man because they did not take the textbook.

2. Miss Crocker expects Mama to be upset once she tells her about Cassie and Little Man. Miss Crocker finds it shocking to see Mama have little emotion. Mama politely thanks her for sharing the news.

3. Mama takes paper and glues it in the book. She does this to cover the derogatory remarks written in the books.

4. As Mama is gluing the paper into the front of all the books, Cassie realizes that Mama feels the same way that she and Little Man do about the textbooks.

Making Connections—Section 1: Chapters 1–3 (page 22)

1. 1922 subtracted from the current year

2. 1933 – 9 = 1924; Excellent

3. 1943 + 5 = 1948; 1948 – 1922 = 26 years old

4. 1861 + 4 = 1865; 1933 – 1865 = 68 years

5. 1970 – 1924 = 46 years old

During-Reading Vocabulary Activity—Section 2 : Chapters 4–5 (page 26)

1. The **proprietor** of the Barnett Mercantile store is always interrupting T.J.'s order because he gives priority to white customers. He makes T.J. wait while he attends to these customers.

2. Stacey **retaliates** by chasing down T.J. after school. He catches him as they near the Wallace store, and they fight each other.

Close Reading the Literature—Section 2: Chapters 4–5 (page 31)

1. The children notice that Mr. Berry is badly disfigured and burned. The book gives a vivid description as to what they see.

2. Members of the Wallace family attacked Mr. Berry and his nephews. The Wallaces poured kerosene on them and set them on fire. One nephew was killed and another is disfigured just as Mr. Berry is.

3. Mama warns the children to stay away from the Wallace store. After the fight between T.J. and Stacey, Mama wants to show the children her reasons for staying away.

4. Answers will vary.

Close Reading the Literature—Section 3: Chapters 6–7 (page 41)

1. Mr. Granger is aware of the Logan's plan to boycott the Wallace store. He is also aware that they are trying to get others to join in on the cause.

2. Uncle Hammer responds with, "Ain't gonna lose it," when Mr. Granger threatens the loss of the land owned by the Logan family.

3. After not getting a response from Pa and Uncle Hammer, Mr. Granger turns his attention to Mama to try and talk some sense into her about the boycott.

4. Papa tells Mr. Granger that he is wasting his time trying to threaten him. Mr. Granger responds with a new threat letting Papa know that the issue with the boycott is not over.

During-Reading Vocabulary Activity— Section 4: Chapters 8–9 (page 46)

1. Cassie asks Lillian Jean to the **glade** to let her know that the last month was all part of her plan. When they arrive, Cassie throws Lillian Jean's books to the ground and then tells her that she will reveal all of her secrets if she lets anyone know about the fight.

2. T.J. contemplates cheating on his **examinations** at school, but decides against it. He then fails these tests and blames Mama for it.

Close Reading the Literature—Section 4: Chapters 8–9 (page 51)

1. When Papa returns from Vicksburg, Mr. Morrison is carrying him in his arms. The family notices he has a broken leg and his head is wrapped with a blood-soaked towel.

2. Stacey feels guilty about Papa's injury because he cannot hold the wagon up while Papa fixes the wheel. The wagon falls and breaks Papa's leg.

3. The book goes into detail about Mr. Morrison's strength in this chapter. He is able to singlehandedly take care of the three men that attack Papa and Stacey while they try to repair the wagon.

4. Answers will vary

Close Reading the Literature—Section 5: Chapters 10–12 (page 61)

1. The children see headlights approaching from the distance. Many angry adults get out and approach T.J's house.

2. The men crawl through the same window that T.J. enters. They exit dragging both parents out the front door, and they push the daughters out through some of the open windows. The men force T.J. out of the house on his knees.

3. Kaleb Wallace accuses T.J. of hurting Mr. and Mrs. Barnett. He also accuses him of stealing the pistol and having two friends as accomplices.

4. Mr. Jamison arrives as a voice of reason to the men attacking T.J. and his family. He tries to convince the men to let the law handle the situation.

Comprehension Assessment (page 67)

1. b. Little Man uses the shovel furiously to help dig a gully that the bus would eventually cross.

2. f. on the side of a road

3. d. It is wrong to treat people unfairly based on the color of their skin.

4. f. "I'm a Southerner, born and bred, but that doesn't mean I approve of all that goes on here, and there are a lot of other white people who feel the same."

5. Main idea—The Logan children are free while their friend T.J. is not.

6. a. Cassie and Little Man would continue their education next fall.
c. Cassie is free to relax near the water and the trees.

7. No matter what happens, don't let anyone bring you down. Push on forward, no matter what.

8. g. Kaleb Wallace